The Little Book on
Dealing with Depression

By Steve Goldblum

Disclaimer: This book is intended to guide people who suffer or are dealing with people who are suffering from depression. **If you are contemplating suicide or thinking of any kind self-harm or causing harm to others around you, then please do contact a medical professional immediately.**

Author can be contacted on Instagram. Handle is @LittleImprovementsDaily

Dedicated to Sushant Singh Rajput, an actor who left us before his time and inspired millions till the very end.

Foreword

I must start this book, as any lawyer would begin an activity, with a disclaimer. The author of this book does not possess any medical degree. *If you are contemplating suicide or thinking of any kind self-harm or causing harm to others around you, then please do contact a medical professional immediately.* The only expertise that I can claim in the field of "depression" (a term that I will define in Chapter 1 of this book) is that I have been a victim of it and managed to overcome it. In the year 2016, I had suddenly become inactive on account of my depression and would regularly experience anxiety attacks. It was at that point of time that I began researching on depression and how to overcome it. With my enhanced knowledge on the subject I was also able to help friends and colleagues combat depression. In 2019, I again began exhibiting symptoms of depression, but because I had a good grasp of the concept, I could identify it and prevent it from becoming severe.

The thought of writing a book on the subject never dawned on me since I was occupied in setting up my own legal practice at the time. Then on 14th June 2020, in the midst of the COVID 19 crisis, news broke out that upcoming Indian actor named Sushant Singh Rajput committed suicide. Rajput did not leave any note explaining the reason for his suicide but those close to him stated that he had been suffering from depression for over six months. A number of celebrities posted their condolences on social media and also expressed their bewilderment as to why the actor took such a drastic step. Some even pointed out the irony that, Rajput had starred in a movie called *'Chhichhore'* in which his character explains the significance of mental health and why one should embrace failure rather than choose to commit suicide. News channels broadcasted Rajput's old interviews and stage performances for several days. His death shook the Indian people, and drew focus on the need to be able to openly discuss our emotions. It was on the immediate next day, i.e. on 15th June 2020 that I began writing this book. The research was already done in the past, so I was able to finish it in three whole days.

Out of respect for the recently deceased, I will not speculate the cause of Sushant Singh Rajput's depression. I will, however, enumerate examples of several famous personalities such as Angelina Jolie, Johnny Depp, Jim Carrey, Dwayne Johnson (The Rock), Buzz Aldrin, etc. who have openly declared that they have suffered at the hands of the villain of this book (– depression) and by examining their cases, set out it's causes and symptoms. I will also extinguish all myths or misconceptions about depression, that is prevalent in society in Chapter 3.

Lastly, in chapter 5 of this book, I will provide the possible solutions that one can try in order to combat their own depression or help a friend or family member (or perhaps even a stranger) overcome their depression. Some of the readers looking for a quick fix might just turn to chapter 5 of this book, but that would not be a wise approach. If one does not have a firm understanding of the meaning and cause of their depression, one runs the risk of a relapse which may, in some cases, be of greater severity.

Readers can also receive a free ebook written by me on sustaining a good diet by entering their email id here: https://forms.gle/eEr1g7FpJwaNAStW7

Table of Contents

Chapter 1: Depression and its Symptoms

What is Depression?

We humans are not intellectual beings. More than 90% of our decisions are based on emotions rather than rational thought or measured consideration. We are slaves to our emotions and while there are means by which we can try and control these feelings and minimalize the impact they have on our actions, we have to ultimately learn to accept them and deal with them in a healthy manner. Depression is one such emotion which sends people into a spiral. A person feeling depression feels bad about themselves which just feeds their depression further, until the cause of depression is overcome.

The primary reason depression is taken lightly is because it is put on the same pedestal as mere 'sadness'. When people feel upset or disappointed, they will often say that they are depressed. Sadness/grief and depression have some common elements but they are by no means the same. The loss of a loved one, or of a job will surely lead to sadness or grief. These emotions are not harmful, and are actually sign of good mental health. Persons experiencing sadness or grief may even temporarily withdraw from some activities that they would usually perform. The fundamental distinctions between these emotions is that depression lasts much longer and in many cases it can also lead to a feeling of worthlessness and self-hatred. Situations which cause grief can also cause depression, and it is possible for one to experience both simultaneously, in which case the period one experiences grief

11

is extended. Sadness is often a symptom of being in a depressed mood, particularly in adults.

Depression is a state of low mood that throws one into despair and causes one to become averse to activity. It has the ability to adversely affect one's thoughts, behavior, and motivations. In extreme cases, and if left unchecked, the victim may also tend to inflict self-harm.

Depression affects an estimated one in 15 adults (6.7%) every year. One in six people (16.6%) will experience depression at some time in their life. Depression can strike at any time, but on average, first appears during the late teens to mid-20s. Depression can affect anyone — even a person who appears to live in relatively ideal circumstances – as I will show by examples in Chapter 4.

Contrary to what most people think, depression is neither a weakness nor an attitude problem. Many medical experts categorize depression as a disease, but I do not find this to be entirely accurate, not in a medical sense but primarily because of the connotation of the word 'disease'. Depression is an illness but may not always be a disease. For the purpose of emphasizing this point I have classified depression into two broad categories:

(i) Depression caused by external factors: This is the kind of depression that arises from life-events, change in social environment, intake of medication or other substances. People who suffer from this kind of depression are supposed to see a psychologist rather than a psychiatrist.

(ii)   Depression arising from mood disorders: In some cases the cause of a depressed mood may simply be a mental disorder. The two most common of such disorders are the Major Depressive Disorder (MDD) and Persistent Depressive Disorder (PDD). MDD is more severe than PDD. People suffering from MDD may perpetually have symptoms of depression present (unless it is treated) or they may have periods of depression separated by years. A person suffering from MDD can often be distinguished from a person who is only in a depressed mood by the fact that the period of depression usually lasts longer than two weeks in the case of MDD. Cause of MDD can be

14

hormonal, genetic or can be a auxiliary to other prevailing health problems. PDD may persist for one or two years and is often characterized by extended periods of depressed mood combined with at least two other symptoms which may include changes in sleep pattern, fatigue or low energy, eating changes (more or less), low self-esteem, or feelings of hopelessness. We need not go in detail into the technical differences between these two disorders. People suffering from a mood disorder are supposed to go see a psychiatrist rather than a psychologist.

Both of the above categories of depression require a different nature of treatment.

The good news is that all kinds of depression are treatable. Some types of treatment are more long term than others. There is no single solution to treat a particular kind of depression, for the human mind is not that simple. The sufferer may have to try different types of treatments, and through the process of trial and error they will eventually find something that works for them. Painful as this may sound, it is the truth, and I assure you that any person who guarantees a 'one-cap-fits-all' solution to depression, is lying.

Symptoms

Symptoms of depression may vary from case to case. Generally, when adults are depressed they become quiet and sad. When a child or teenager is depressed they will, more often than not, be more irritable ad aggressive. Younger sufferers of depression are more likely to display disturbances in eating and sleep patterns. They also experience physical pains or aches which do not disappear with normal remedies meant to treat physical pains or injuries. Other symptoms of depression include:

- Anhedonia, (i.e. loss of interest or a loss of feeling of pleasure in certain activities that usually bring joy to people). This is one of the most common symptoms of depression.
- Sadness
- Difficulty in thinking and lack of concentration
- Feeling of dejection, hopelessness or suicidal thoughts

- Loss or increase of appetite
- Increase or decrease in time spent sleeping or a change in sleep pattern
- Loss of energy or increased fatigue
- Slow movements or speech
- Increase in purposeless activities, such as pacing around a room or fidgeting
- Feeling worthless
- Dark thoughts, particularly regarding death or suicide

The above symptoms can vary from mild to severe. Symptoms must last at least two weeks for a medical diagnosis of depression. However, if caught earlier than that the sufferer or her/his friends and family members can take steps to prevent it from getting more severe.

None of the above symptoms by themselves are an indication of depression. I would say that if you suffer from at least three of the symptoms simultaneously it is sufficient to say that you suffer from at least a mild, if not sever, depression.

Chapter 2: Causes of Depression

Depression can be caused by any one of the below, or a combination of them.

Brain Chemicals and Hormonal Imbalance

Like the symptoms of depression, even causes of depression may vary. Some believe that depression is merely a result of a hormonal imbalance or an imbalance of chemicals in the brain known as 'neurotransmitters'. This cause cannot be ruled out. A change in our social surroundings may not cause any type of comprehendible stress or disappointment, yet a person may show signs of depression. The release of hormones is very much dependent on our conscious and sub-conscious thoughts, which have the ability cause our brains to send signals which ultimately lead to release of certain hormones. This is the reason why the cause of our depression is not always evident to us. This is also the reason that psychologists attempt delve into the sub-conscious of a patient suffering from depression to find the root of the problem.

Neurotransmitters are basically the chemicals that facilitate the carrying of messages between neurons. The neurotransmitter called 'serotonin' is important when we talk about depression. When serotonin is low it can lead to depression in an individual.

Genetics

In some cases it is observed that depression is hereditary. A person whose parents suffer from mood disorders is two to three times more likely to develop the disorder. Buzz Aldrin, the second man to lay his feet on the moon suffered at the hands of alcohol and depression after the successful Apollo mission. His mother and maternal grandfather had both committed suicide, and Aldrin believes that he inherited the alcoholism and depression in his genes. Aldrin has undergone treatment and is currently chairman of the National Mental Health Association.

External Factors

The last cause is perhaps the most important – a persons environment and their emotional quotient.

The most common external factor that leads to depression is stress. Stress is good in small quantities. It ensures that we remain on track and are able to meet deadlines. Without a small amount of stress we tend to have lackadaisical attitude, which is also not desirable. But it is important to ensure that our stress levels do not cross a limit, beyond which it can have negative effects on our mental and physical health. There is a quote by Prof. Xavier from the movie X-men First Class which may be relevant here: 'True focus lies somewhere between rage and serenity'. Similarly, true focus can be achieved when there is a small to moderate amount of stress. The same it is with stress. Little keeps us motivated, too much causes us to breakdown.

Loss or grief or failure are the next biggest external factors. It is okay to grieve for the loss of a loved one, or when a relationship is broken off. But it is not okay to wallow in our despair. Life moves on. Failure is important in life too. Do not despair over the loss of a job or the failure of a start-up. Edison wasn't able to make a light bulb in his first attempt. He is often attributed for having said that he didn't fail in the first 1,000 attempts, he just found 1,000 ways that did not work. The mistakes we make is what hones us. Failure is the best teacher and our duty is to be a good student, learn from our mistakes and try again. I, myself, spent a year studying for an examination that I was unable to clear. I felt I wasted my time and the feeling of worthlessness dawned on me. It was at the same time that I faced rejection from dozens of firms. I also faced relationship problems. Over three years have passed since then, and I am at a good place in my profession, am happily married and am in peace with myself. Life events feel very huge in the moment, but the bad moments pass. Life is long and our memories fade with time, or if not fade, our ability to live and cope with them improves.

A person suffering from a physical illness might also feel depressed because of their physical ailment or handicap. One of my schoolmates lost his arm in a train accident He was depressed for a very long time. Thanks to family and friends he was able to overcome it and cleared his Bachelors in Arts and is living a happy life. A quote by Dr. Stephen Hawking is very worth remembering: 'However bad life may seem, there is always something you can do and succeed at. Where there's life, there's hope.' Hawking also posted the following on social media: *"Although I'm severely disabled, I have been successful in my scientific work. I travel widely and have been to Antarctica and Easter Island, down in a submarine and up on a zero gravity flight. ....I've been privileged to gain some understanding of the way the universe operates through my work. But it would be an empty universe indeed without the people that I love."*

It might be important to point out here that life is not one-dimensional, but we sometimes choose to make it so. Life is not only our career or only our family or only our friends, or only our life-partner. Career is a *part* of life. Our life partner is a *part* of our life. When we acknowledge that every aspect of our life is only a part of our life and not our life in whole, we are able to cope with hurdles that occur in those particular parts.

Trauma or abuse can take a toll on us which can follow us for the rest of our lives. I have myself been a victim of domestic abuse in my childhood, which has effects on my personality till date. I can let those events decide all my future decisions and behaviour or I can try to overcome it. There is still a lot of stuff I am going through because of those traumatic incidents but they usually pass quickly and don't effect my work or my relations. My reading on stoicism played a huge role here. The stoics accept the fact that a lot of events in our lives cannot be controlled. Instead of hoping for an ideal society, a stoic tries to see the world as it is while pursuing self-improvement through four cardinal virtues:-

(i)   practical wisdom: gaining knowledge and information which will enable us to navigate complex situations in a logical and informed manner;

(ii)   temperance: exercising self-restraint and moderation in all aspects of life;

(iii) justice, being fair yet merciful and forgiving to our friends and family; and

(iv)   courage: not just in extraordinary situations, but facing our day to day challenges instead of avoiding them.

I highly recommend reading the book Man's Search for Meaning (1946) by Viktor Frankl which chronicles his experiences as a prisoner in Nazi concentration camps during World War II and how he still managed to find a positive purpose in life and avoid depression. I also recommend googling quotes on stoicism, since many of them are quite inspiring. If you find them useful you can read more about stoicism.

Personality

People who lack self-confidence or self-esteem or who easily become anxious or stressed, or who are just pessimistic by nature, are more likely to suffer depression. These personality traits by themselves do not cause depression, but only trigger or amplify the causes already mentioned above. For this reason I hesitate to mention personality as a cause of depression, but it is a factor that can increase the likelihood or severity of depression.

Some people keep dwelling on disappointing or embarrassing events in their lives, while some are better at moving on. Those who dwell on thoughts fall into depression more easily and find it harder to come out of it.

Nihilism: Sometimes depression can arise because of a certain kind of belief, or lack of it. Existential nihilism leads one to believe that life is without objective meaning, purpose, or value. An existential crisis may lead one to cause self-harm or harm to others. This proves to be a tricky situation since it is difficult to come up with a cogent argument that can convince a nihilist. Nihilism is a non-philosophy. Philosophy helps you understand about the meaning of life and how it is to be lived. Existential nihilism tells you that life is meaningless while moral nihilism tells you that morals are of no value in life.

I recall a quote of the Greek philosopher Diogenes who recounts a story of another philosopher Thales of Miletus: "Thales said there was no difference between life and death. "Why, then," said someone to him, "do not you die?" "Because," said he, "it does make no difference."

Thus, our approach when dealing with nihilism shouldn't be to make arguments as to why life has meaning (although there is no harm in trying to do so), but rather that their life in particular is worth living. The fact that life is temporary is what makes it worth a damn. True, that we live on a tiny speck on a small solar system, in a vast galaxy surrounded by other vast galaxies, in a universe which is billions of years old and which will probably last for trillions of years more and maybe one day end as it began – with a big bang. It doesn't matter that there is no blackboard in the sky where it is written that what we our purpose in life is. We give our own life purpose. We achieve as much as we can. We enjoy each day as much as we can. We try to bring joy to others and assist our society when possible. To paraphrase Mahatma Gandhi: 'Whatever you do will be insignificant, but it is very important that you do it.' Every dot in an impressionist painting is significant. Our existence may seem circular – we exist in order to continue the existence of mankind. But in reality we exist in order to feel. To feel joy, sadness, empathy and feelings that our limited language cannot describe.

The fact that death will inevitably come to us is, in fact, good. There will come a day when our mistakes or failures will be left in the mortal world, and thus they are insignificant in the grand scheme of things. While we are living, the most we can do is make sure that we make as little mistakes as possible, and try to correct any wrongs we may have done in the past, to ensure that we do not die with any regrets.

Gender

Women get depressed twice as often as men. But the disparity is prominent among people in the age group of 12 to 40. That means this disparity is not evident in children and older adults. So, it might be safe to conclude that the hormonal differences are what causes this disparity. Estrogen and progesterone, the female reproductive hormones have a major effect depression. Research states that women are more prone to depression during the premenstrual depression, right after childbirth and in the period surrounding menopause.

That being said, I don't want to undermine depression in men. Since childhood it has been instilled in us that men do not cry. Men do not feel pain. Men are not sensitive. Because of these lies, men never discuss their emotions openly. They conform with society's expectation from them that they ought to keep their emotions bottled up. This is also the reason that men have little or no people with whom they can be open. They try to experiment with a few friends, but immediately regret their decision when they see the judgment in their friend's eyes and in their responses.

Chapter 3: Society and Depression

Society and me

I am always astounded by how little people discuss mental health issues, despite the ever-increasing rate of suicide. In 2016, suicide was the most common cause of death in India. Our mental health encompasses our psychological, emotional and social well-being. This means it impacts how we feel, think and behave each day. Our mental health also contributes to our decision-making process, how we cope with stress and how we relate to others in our lives.

Mental health issues ought to be taken as seriously as any physical illness. It is sad to see that depression, a condition that is very much treatable, is one of the leading causes for suicide in world. Every now and then a well-known personality commits suicide. People are shocked. The media will go on about it for days. Some people will post about the importance of mental health. People who knew the personality personally will say things like "If only I had detected it in time." Or "If only I knew the pain you were going through." Then, time passes and while some of the close family and friends still grieve her/his death, but they will ignore other people around them exhibiting symptoms of depression.

I would be remiss if I didn't point out that the lyrics of the song 'How to Save a Life' by The Fray is very much on point. The song is based on a boy who was attending a camp for troubled teenagers. This boy had lost his best friend was not able to cope with the loss. He was losing friends and going through depression. The song describes an attempt by an adult to confront this teen. In the chorus, the singer laments that he himself was unable to save his friend because he did not know how to do so. This is the case with most members of society. Most of us have the tools to help someone who is suffering from depression. I'm not saying that we should try to take up treatment ourselves, but we are capable of giving moral support, of uplifting the sufferer and making the sufferer realize that professional help is available and effective.

Because of society, I was always afraid to open up about my own emotions. Firstly, I was born in a country where mental health issues is a taboo topic and going to a therapist is something one must never even contemplate, lest other members of society find out and my family's reputation be soiled. Seeing a therapist has not yet become as common here as it has in the western countries.

Secondly, I had suffered a large amount of abuse and bullying in my childhood, which had left me with emotional scars which I carry to this day. Those childhood incidents left me emotionally crippled and unable to cope with my feelings. I am often attributed as being a very robotic person and some people who I worked with have in the past told me on my face that they do not think that I'm emotional at all. The truth is that I have always been extremely sensitive and emotional, but have become unable to express it. Another reason people had this misconception about me is because I always carried a polite smile on my face regardless of the circumstances. In actuality, carrying a smile at all times was a habit I had practiced in order to mask my emotions. And this is where another important point comes in – Just because someone is calm, composed or even smiling, does not mean they are not depressed! You really must observe the subtleties in the change in someone's behaviour in order to realize it.

Thirdly, I was born in a middle-class family who did not know how to deal with depression. Ironically, in some conservative families, if a child mentions that he wants to see a therapist, the parents would give him a look as if he is suffering from a mental disorder – the disorder being that s/he wants to see a therapist. They will convince the child to talk to them instead. Let me clarify, that it very much encouraged that you let your child know that you are there in case he needs to talk. But you must never insist that your child talk to you instead of talking to a professional. Not only does it put the child in an awkward position, but the child will never come forth again to ask for help.

Thus, in 2016, I had to deal with my depression all by myself. At the time of writing this book I can happily say that my wife is now always there to hear me out. Although she herself is not proficient in dealing with depression, she does make a genuine effort, and that is something I always appreciate. There are a few things that she says, which are phrases you must never utter in front of a depressed person. In the final chapter of this book I have mentioned a list of things one must never say to a person suffering from depression.

A revolution in mental health is coming. Maybe not today, maybe not tomorrow, but soon enough. Call me an optimist, but I see a future where students in schools are thought about depression, where every educational institution and mid to large-sized corporation would be required by law to have a full-time therapist for the students, teachers and office staff, where both men and women are encouraged to openly talk about their feelings without fear of judgement, where a person suffering from depression knows that help is available and is treated before being able to take any drastic steps. In addition there is one more thing I really wish to see in this new society - that bullying and raging would be concepts which people would know about simply by descriptions in books and would never experience first-hand.

Myths

There are several preconceived notions that members of society have about depression. These are just some of the most common myths:

- *Depression is the same as being sad.*

41

- *Depression is only caused by a traumatic event.* In reality the cause of depression many a times not detectable. The sufferer may herself/himself think that s/he is effected by a minor event, when in actuality the cause for their depression is a combination of factors/events.
- *Depression is a sign of weakness*
- *Depression is not an illness*
- *Depression is something mostly women go through.* This doesn't explain why the suicide rate is higher in men. Not that depression is always the cause of suicide, but it is the most common cause. The reason this myth exists is because society frowns at men who talk about their emotions. Because of this "man box" they are put into, they have to suffer in silence.

- *Successful and rich people do not get depressed.* Robin Williams and Elvis Presley were both victims of depression while still at the peak of their careers.
- *Depression disappears on its own with time*
- *Depression can be cured by medication in every case.* In some cases medication is the answer in some it is not.
- *Talking about depression only makes it worse.*

Chapter 4: Famous Personalities who Overcame their Depression

I will now set out examples of some famous personalities who suffered depression but were able to successfully combat it. I have only briefly touched upon their stories, and if the case of any particular personality resonates with the reader, I urge you to study it in-detail.

Angelina Jolie: She has been one of most vocal Hollywood celebrities when it comes to battling with mental illness. Her depression took her to such a dark place that she has even cut herself and once hired a hit man to kill her. Despite a successful career in 2007 she again fell into depression following the loss of her mother to cancer. In order to come out of her depression she threw herself into her work and accepted a lead role in the movie "Wanted". She once said "I felt I was going into a very dark place, and I wasn't capable of getting up in the morning, so I signed up for something that would force me to be active."

Dwayne Johnson: The wrestler-turned-actor admits having suffered from depression. He once tweeted "Depression never discriminates. Took me a long time to realize it but the key is to not be afraid to open up. Especially us dudes have a tendency to keep it in. You're not alone."

Deepika Padukone: The actress had suffered depression despite already being a huge success in the Indian film industry. Fortunately, her mother spotted her symptoms in time and urged her to seek professional help. In 2020, during her acceptance speech at the "Crystal Award" ceremony at the World Economic Forum annual meeting in Davos, she said that learning to understand what she was experiencing was the first step to recovery, Padukone said. She encouraged potential sufferers and the people around them to look out for tell-tale signs of depression, such as prolonged feelings of sadness, sleeping and eating irregularities, as well as suicidal thoughts. The toughest part in the journey for me was not understanding what I was feeling," said Padukone. "Just having the diagnoses in itself felt like a massive relief." In 2015, she set up the Live, Love, Laugh Foundation in 2015 to support other sufferers.

Kristen Bell: On an interview on the 'Off-Camera Show', Bell disclosed that she has been taking medication for her depression and anxiety which were caused due to a serotonin imbalance. She was well aware that there was no shame in admitting her

46

depression or taking medication for it. She said "You would never deny a diabetic his insulin, but for some reason when someone needs a serotonin inhibitor, they're immediately crazy or something."

Jim Carrey: In an interview with 60 Minutes, Carrey admitted he has spent much of his life dealing with depression. After his second marriage also failed, he began seeing a psychiatrist who prescribed him Prozac. He said in the interview that he had realized that he didn't want to be on the drug forever together. He said "I had to get off [the Prozac] at a certain poin…You need to get out of bed every day and say that life is good. That's what I did, although at times it was very difficult for me." Carrey says that a healthy diet and natural supplements has improved his mental health.

Lady Gaga: In an interview with Billboard, she said "I've suffered through depression and anxiety my entire life. I just want these kids to know that ... I learned that my sadness never destroyed what was great about me. You just have to go back to that greatness, find that one little light that's left. I'm lucky I found one little glimmer stored away." Lady Gaga is now a strong advocate for mental health. One of the missions of her Born This Way Foundation is to help young people deal with depression and severe anxiety.

Johnny Depp: The versatile actor clearly shows signs of depression when seen off-screen. In order to cope with this it is said that Depp requires access to therapists at all times, including on set.

J.K. Rowling: One must read about this women and the struggles she faced before the success of the Harry Potter series. She has experienced poverty, an unemployed single mother and spent her days writing in local cafes not knowing if her work will ever be successful. She was also suffering from severe depression and battling suicidal thoughts. Rowling even underwent cognitive behavior therapy in an attempt to improve her condition. She is fine now (or at least seems so, for it is impossible to tell from afar) Her dark thoughts inspired the fictional creatures known as 'Dementors', which feed off of the happiness of people in the Harry Potter series.

Eminem: In his memoir, The Way I Am, the rapper describes his battle with depression. In 2006 his close friend and D12 member was murdered. His relationship with his now ex-wife was rocky. Eminem states, "I have never felt so much pain in my life. It was tough for me to even get out of bed and I had days when I couldn't walk, let alone write a rhyme."

Jon Hamm: The star of the TV show 'Mad Men', has had his fair share of struggles with depression. Therapy helped him come out of it. In an interview for a magazine he said "We live in a world where to admit anything negative about yourself is seen as a weakness, when it's actually a strength. It's not a weak move to say, 'I need help.'"

Reese Witherspoon: The Legally Blonde actress suffered depression after her divorce in 2007. Fortunately, she had close friends who helped her cope with it. "[They] came over, stood me up, put me in the shower, put my clothes on, took my kids to school, brought me dinner" she said.

You may find some of the above stories inspiring, and most of them are. But like a movie villain who rises once the overconfident hero has turned his back, depression can come back at any time. The above personalities have slayed it one or more times, but yet it can come back again. The important thing is to remember how to deal with it in a healthy manner and ensure that it does not consume us.

Chapter 5: Depression Management

Managing Depression

Depression is a real illness and help is easily available. Fortunately, depression is one of the most treatable mental disorders. Between 80 percent and 90 percent of people with depression recover with treatment and almost all patients gain some kind of relief.

Thus, with proper diagnosis and treatment, the vast majority of people with depression can eliminate it. If you are experiencing symptoms of depression, a first step is to see your family physician or psychiatrist. Talk about your concerns and request a thorough evaluation. I will now set out some of the steps you can try in order to combat depression:

a) Diet

More than 60% of dry weight of the brain is made up of fat. There was a time when 'fats' had gained a bad reputation. Fortunately, it is now well established that there are good fats and bad fats. Even those on Keto diet try to eat food rich with the good fats while avoiding carbs. One of the best type of fats is a group called Omega-3 fatty acids. Several different types of omega-3s exist, but the majority of scientific research focuses on three: alpha-linolenic acid (ALA), eicosapentaenoic acid (EPA), and docosahexaenoic acid (DHA). ALA is present in plant oils, such as flaxseed, soybean, and canola oils. DHA and EPA are present in fish and fish oils. Other foods which are rich in omega-3s are nuts, seeds and leafy vegetables. You'll notice that these are foods which are ancestors usually ate. That's why the paleo diet gained popularity.

Omega-3 supplements are being used to treat depression these days. I'm not saying that a change in diet itself can get rid of depression. But in combination with other treatments it can do miracles for you. Even if you aren't focusing on omega-3s its important to Eat healthy. Avoid junk food and sugar till your depression goes away. It is okay to have a cheat meal once a week. But don't binge!

To receive a free ebook on Sustaining a Good Diet enter your email id here: https://forms.gle/eEr1g7FpJwaNAStW7

b) Physical Exercise

Physical exercise works better than most of the common anti-depressant. The brain chemicals such as dopamine and serotonin released during physical exercise help in combating depression. During depression the brain's production of the hormone called BNDF reduces substantially. This can cause the brain to start shrinking and cause learning and memory problems. Exercise counters this and increased the production of BNDF.

Physical exercise doesn't mean going to the gym. But just playing an outdoor sport, or going for a jog or a brisk walk, particularly in the mornings, can release the right hormones and make a depressed person feel better. Brisk walking did wonders for my own depression. I actually signed up for a few marathons as well, not for any competitive reason of course, but just to feel better and get fit.

There were also some good diet tips that I got from the book 'Ikigai'. One of them is that instead of eating one or two dishes in large quantity, you should have a little bit of six to seven items of different colours. Variety is the spice of life. Basically, your aim should be to get all, or as many as possible, colours of the rainbow in your meal consisting of items of different levels of acidity and different types. The Indian *thali* is the good example of this, except for the fact that most people tend to have too much rice or *chapatti* instead of focusing on the vegetables and other healthy foods.

c) Meditation

In its simplest form meditation is only a person sitting in a spot, with her/his body relaxed and trying to rid the mind of conscious thought. How does one do that? Well, obviously some thoughts will keep coming in your mind, but the important thing is to swipe them away as soon as they pop up. Do not indulge in any thought! Do not even focus on your breathing, for even thinking about your breathing is a thought. You need not achieve nirvana, but this kind of meditation itself will help you control your thoughts and how to deal with particular thoughts without passing judgement on yourself.

d) Avoid indulgence in negative thoughts

It's good to reflect on the past to learn from our mistakes but if you catch yourself constantly thinking about a negative thought, you should quickly end it. I know this is like telling a person to not think of elephants, and actually expecting them to not think about elephants. But this is where your meditation will pay off. If you still can't control your thoughts then you should try to focus on something else every time you catch yourself thinking about negative thoughts. You can try doing some light exercise or doing something productive at these times.

e) Let there be light!

Do you notice how some people tend to feel more depressed during cloudy days or during seasons when there is less sunlight. The human body has an internal clock which relies heavily on the body's exposure to sunlight.

Artificial light is okay, but it doesn't compare to natural sunlight. You will notice how this works well with your brisk walking and jogging. You can get natural sunlight while doing these physical exercises. If you can jog in a park or garden you are also exposed to nature and this 'trifecta' will be great for you.

Even when you aren't able to get exposure to natural sunlight, make sure you at least that you are exposed to a good amount of artificial lighting during your waking hours. You should only be darkness during sleeping hours.

f) Sleep

Depression causes disturbances in sleep and disturbances in sleep schedule. Try your best to stick to the sleep schedule that you followed before your depression disturbed it. Bad sleep hygiene can amplify the effects of depression. We all know that you need a minimum amount of sleep, being 6-8 hours a day, to maintain our mental and physical health. However, over-sleeping can be equally hazardous. When you over sleep you get less done during the day and you tend to feel worse, thus amplifying your depression.

Quality of sleep is also important so ensure that factors such as darkness, air quality, noise, etc. are conducive to sleeping.

g) Communicate

Talk to people who are close to you and with whom you can share your thoughts and feelings without judgment from them. If you do not have any such people in your life, there are several foundations that help people feeling depressed. You can also consider seeing a therapist. If you get a fever or headache, you go to a doctor, then why not go to a therapist when you are facing a mental illness?

Psychotherapy, or "talk therapy," is sometimes used alone for treatment of mild depression; for moderate to severe depression, psychotherapy is often used in along with antidepressant medications. Psychotherapy usually involves only the sufferer, but it can include others. For example, family or couples therapy can help address issues within these close relationships. Group therapy involves people with similar illnesses, but is not suggested for depression, which is more case specific.

For people who cannot afford a therapist, I have something that worked for me. There was a website called www.7cups.com in which you can anonymously chat with volunteers, called 'listeners' who are willing to hear you out. The volunteers aren't usually trained therapists, so you can just treat them as friends who you can be absolutely open with since they don't know your identity. This website did wonders for me since I had someone who I could talk with openly. After a few years I volunteered as a listener myself and started helping out depressed people anonymously. The response and gratitude I got from strangers was re-affirming.

h) Schedule

Make a schedule for your sleep, exercise and other activities and stick to it! Self-discipline is necessary for combating depression. If you happen to not follow your schedule, on a particular day, don't feel to bad, just don't let a day convert into a series of days or binge on a single activity.

Plan your week and keep a to-do list. The rush you get from crossing things off your to-do list is the good kind of rush.

i) Social Media

Dopamine is good, but not in the manner that we try to get the same from social media. Seeking cheap pleasure from social media and being addicted to it is no different from over-indulging in masturbation. Both are okay in small quantities but in too much in a week is harmful and makes us depressed.

On social media you see the best parts of people's lives. Everyone is happy all the time and celebrating a milestone in their lives. You would think that these people have rainbows coming out of their butts, if you didn't know them personally. In reality you know that nobody's life is as perfect as it seems on social media. Everyone has problems. A lot of people struggle or feel depressed. Happiness doesn't come without sacrifice. But when you expose yourself to the happiness without exposing yourself to the sacrifice and the pain that comes along with you tend to, sub-consciously or consciously, think that other people are only having highs without lows in their lives. This makes us feel much worse.

This doesn't mean that you should hangout with people who are not doing so well and avoid people who are in a good place in their lives. But on social media we are flooded with this phenomenon of in copious quantities, which should be avoided at all costs.

j)   Medication and Behaviour Therapy

If nothing else works out, then do go see a psychiatrist. If they feel necessary, they will prescribe medication or alternate forms of therapy. Medication will be prescribed when the problem arises due to a problem in Brain chemistry or hormonal imbalance.

Before a diagnosis or treatment, the expert will conduct a thorough diagnostic evaluation, including an interview and maybe a physical examination. The expert will try to identify specific symptoms, medical and family history, cultural factors and environmental factors to arrive at a diagnosis and plan a course of action. It is important to let the medical professional know if any medication prescribed is not working or if you are experiencing side effects.

Electroconvulsive Therapy (ECT) is a medical treatment most commonly used for patients with severe major depression or bipolar disorder who have not responded to other treatments. It involves a brief electrical stimulation of the brain while the patient is under anesthesia.

Cognitive behavioral therapy (CBT) has been found to be effective in treating depression. CBT helps a person to recognize distorted thinking and then change behaviors and thinking.

k) Avoid Intoxication and Smoking

Quitting cigarettes and alcohol, or any kind of intoxicated drug, not prescribed by a medical professional can do wonders for your mental health.

l) Embrace the lifestyle changes

The aim of improving your dietary habits, exercising or sticking to a schedule should not be just to overcome your depression. You have to acknowledge that these lifestyle changes are necessary permanent habits and are good for your long term well being as well.

Good habits are important for overall mental well-being. In the short term your goal must be to follow the schedule for only 21 days. But after the 21 days are over, you yourself will know why it is important to continue with those habits.

m) Music

I wouldn't suggest death-metal here. Search "Zen music" on YouTube. Maybe even Beethoven or Mozart will work better for you. If you are close to nature, then the sound of nature itself is sometimes therapeutic.

You can listen to the music while travelling or while you aren't doing any other activity. But the important thing is to ensure that you don't engage into any negative thoughts while listening to the music. Best way to do this is to focus on the music while the same is being played and appreciate it.

n) Nature

Go for a trek if possible. Or else just roam around a nearby park.

Keep a plant at home and nurture it like living being deserves to be. Play music to it, water it daily and treat it like a pet.

o) Hobbies

Engaging in hobbies can help you combat depression. Here are some hobbies that work best:

i.   Horticulture (Gardening)

ii.   Photography

iii.   Learn an instrument

iv.   Writing

v.   Arts such as drawing or painting or sculpting

vi.   Crafts such as knitting, sewing, origami, kirigami, etc.

vii.   Dancing

viii.   Swimming

ix.   Sports such as tennis, football, etc.

x.   Hiking or trekking

xi.   Cooking

p) Acknowledge Mistakes

If your depression has caused you to hurt someone else, you must apologize to them and make it up to them.

q) Be in the moment

Whatever you are doing, be completely immersed in it. When eating food, don't watch TV but savour the food. If you are washing the dishes, enjoy the sound of water and the feel of the scrubbing action. Exercising 'Mindfulness' through all your is good for mental health. This is probably why Bill and Melinda Gates choose to do the dishes themselves!

What You Shouldn't Say to the Sufferer

- You shouldn't tell people suffering from depression that they should 'get over it'. Imagine if your leg were to be That would be like telling a person who's leg was amputated that they should 'get over it'

- Telling a depressed person to "think positive", without fully understanding their voes, is making small of their illness and places blame on the person struggling with the disease. Statements similar to "Count your blessings" or also have the same problems.

- "It's all in your head"

- Don't say "I know how you feel". Instead just explain your case of depression and follow it by a solution as to how you coped. But do not hijack the conversation.

- "It could be worse" makes the sufferer feel ashamed for feeling depressed.

- "You are just craving attention" or "You're such a drama-queen/king"
- "No one ever said life was fair"
- "You don't look depressed" When someone tells you they are depressed you don't get to say that they aren't.
- "Stop feeling sorry for yourself"
- "Stop whining"
- "I thought you were stronger than that"
- "Don't be so weak"

What You Can Say to the Sufferer

- How can I help you during this difficult time?
- I'm sorry that you're hurting.
- I'm here for you.
- I'm sorry is there anything that I can do to help?

- Tell me more about what's going on

- Would you like to take a walk with me?

- Want to grab a cup of coffee together?

- Can we spend some time together today?

- Your feelings are valid.

- Thank you for sharing this with me so that I can understand what you're going through.

Over Self-Help

Lastly, I must warn you that over-reading about depression can also amplify depression. Do your research, by all means, but if it depresses you further, just stop! In November 2015 the *Mint* published an article which said that self-help books can cause depression. I'm setting out an extract of the book below:

"A study shows people who read self-help books are more likely to feel depressed. Researchers from a Canadian institute carried out a small study involving 30 adult men and women, where 18 had read four self-help books of some sort in the last one year. They divided them into four groups according to the type of self-help books they read or did not read. Tests were carried out to measure their salivary cortisol levels, personality and depressive symptoms. They found that stress level was higher in those users who read growth-oriented books that give advice on how to change life, attain happiness or find true love. The group that read problem solving books like how to lose weight showed even higher symptoms of depression. The study was published in the journal Neural Plasticity."

I Value Your Feedback

I am really interested in knowing what you thought about this book. If you found this book helpful then please write a review on Amazon.

You can also message me on Instagram. My handle is @LittleImprovementsDaily

If you feel anything said in this book is incorrect, please let me know. I will re-analyse it and change it if required. The reason for writing this book is to help as many people as possible.

Printed in Great Britain
by Amazon

65023864R00045